B♭ Clarinet

Intermediate Level

MASTER SOLOS
by Ramon Kireilis
EDITED by Linda Rutherford

T0033958

Contents

To access companion recorded performances
and accompaniments online, visit:
www.halleonard.com/mylibrary
Enter Code
3880-2822-5746-9460

ISBN 978-0-7935-9548-8

HAL•LEONARD®

Visit Hal Leonard Online at
www.halleonard.com

Contact Us:
Hal Leonard
7777 West Bluemound Road
Milwaukee, WI 53213
Email: info@halleonard.com

In Europe contact:
Hal Leonard Europe Limited
42 Wigmore Street
Marylebone, London, W1U 2RN
Email: info@halleonardeurope.com

In Australia contact:
Hal Leonard Australia Pty. Ltd.
4 Lentara Court
Cheltenham, Victoria, 3192 Australia
Email: info@halleonard.com.au

Gymnopédie No. 1

musical terms

lent   **slow**
et douloureux   **and mournful**

Hailed as the spiritual guide of a group of younger Parisian composers known as "Les Six" (Honneger, Milhaud, Durey, Tailleferre, Auric, and Poulenc), Erik Satie is remembered more for his influence on his contemporaries than for his few compositions.

The Three Gymnopedies for piano are some of his earliest and best known works. Satie's renewed popularity is due to the arrangement of his piece for flute by the group, Blood, Sweat and Tears. It is characteristic of his style: simple harmonies, melodies and polyphonic textures.

Gymnopedies were ceremonial choral dances performed at ancient Greek festivals. The use of early forms of the Classical Period and the simplistic approach to the music, a reaction to the emotionalism of late Romanticism, led to Neo-Classicism. Satie's compositions were considered trifling and shallow, but his wit and satire were later recognized as his statement against Romanticism and Impressionism.

In each of the solos in this book, you'll see markings like . . . MM ♩=74. The M.M. stands for Maelzel's Metronome, the inventor of the metronome. This particular marking means that the metronome should be set at 74 and each click represents the length of a quarter note.

These indications are suggestions of a tempo. If at first you cannot play the solo at this tempo, practice it slower and gradually increase the speed as you learn it. If this tempo is too fast for you and your accompanist to perform well, play it at a speed that is comfortable for both of you.

In this arrangement you will be working in a key that you probably have not used often. You also will be playing long, controlled phrases. Practice the following scales and arpeggios in E major. Be sure to use the correct fingerings to avoid sliding the little fingers of either hand. Start practicing the scales and arpeggios slowly and evenly, then gradually increase the speed. Check the new fingerings before you begin.

New fingerings for high C♯, D♯, E, F♯

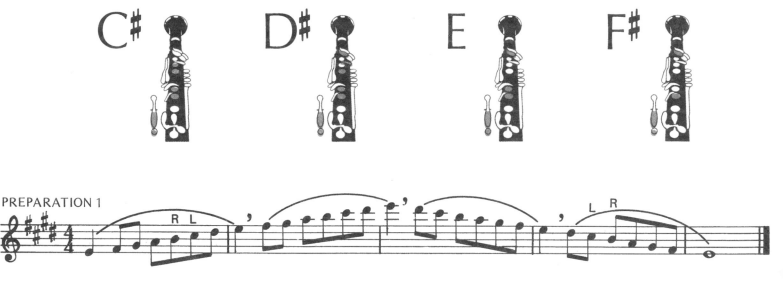

PREPARATION 1

PREPARATION 2

PREPARATION 3

Breath support and long tones are the second area you need to develop more fully. It may help to think of the waist area as the bottom of a balloon. The throat and lips are similar to the neck and lip of the balloon. As air is allowed to escape from the balloon (lungs), the air is forced out by pressure all around the balloon. For you, it is not only the diaphragm muscle that creates the pressure, but all of the muscles around your waist area, sides, back and front.

Each time you practice begin by holding a long tone. By keeping a record of the time, you can increase the length and build your breath support. Another exercise you may want to try uses a lit candle. Stand back from the candle, blow a thin stream of air toward the flame. You should blow as evenly and long as possible to almost blow out the flame. Each time you try this, move back a little farther.

Measure 1-4   Your accompanist will set the mood and tempo for the solo in the four measures of introduction. The musical term, Lent et douloureux, indicates that it should be played slowly and mournfully. The entire solo should be very calm and serene with subdued dynamics and articulations.

Measure 5-8   Be prepared for the first G♯ by thinking of the pitch before you are to begin. Take your breath early enough so the note will not explode. This begins the first phrase of the solo. Use a slight crescendo in the next three measures to help the melody move forward. All your fingerings should be worked out for smoothness. For instance, in measures 6 and 7 and several other places in the solo, the "D♯" to "C♯" has a special pattern using the right little finger and then the left little finger. It may be best to use the right little finger on the "B" in measure 8.

Measure 9-12   The throat "G♯" in these four measures tends to be a little sharp and unclear. Try putting down some of the fingers of your right hand to help lower the pitch and make the tone clearer. You should experiment with different combinations to find which produces the best tone on your instrument. Be sure to take a quick breath before measure 9 so that you can sustain this note for the four measures.

Measure 13-16   Again be prepared for the "G♯" that starts the second phrase. In measure 16 the left little finger is the best choice of fingering due to the "D♯" that follows in measure 17. The note sequence changes in this phrase so the decrescendo will have to be longer.

Measure 22-26   With the introduction of a new key and new thematic material, you should use a little more sound than you used at the beginning. Be careful that with the increase of sound, you don't increase the speed. In measures 23 and 24 use the right little finger for the "C♯".

Measure 27-31   Measure 27-31 is the second phrase in the new key. It should be played at a slightly higher dynamic level than the first phrase. This will keep the melodic line moving forward.

Measure 31-35   Take a full breath in this measure — it has to last for six measures. The "E" in measure 31 must lead in to the "A". Keep the dynamic level full and crescendo slightly when moving from the "E" to the "A". This is the high point of the solo.

In measure 34 there is a particular fingering problem. Because of the melodic line, you must change from the right little finger to the left little finger on the "C♯" on beat 3 in measure 34. Study and practice the example below. Remember: Think of the last "C♯" in measure 34 as two eighth notes tied together, move your little fingers, but don't tongue the notes. Practice this passage until the transition is smooth and no change in the sound can be heard on the third beat.

PREPARATION 4

Measure 40-43   During the measures of rest, take some long breaths. If your instrument has any moisture in the mouthpiece, try to draw it out without making too much noise.

Measure 44-78   From measure 44 to measure 78 the first section is repeated. Keep in mind the points discussed at the beginning. Work out any fingering patterns in this section individually and slowly before playing with the accompanist.

Measure 77-78   Be sure to take a quick breath before this measure so you can get a clear tone in the last two measures. In measure 78 imagine that there is another measure following. The note will then seem to fade away instead of being cut-off.

Gymnopédie No.1

Erik Satie
(1866-1925)

Etude No. 3

musical terms

moderato	moderate speed
espressivo	with expression
con moto	with motion, slightly faster
poco	little
Tempo I	return to original tempo

new notes

The name Baermann is widely associated with the relatively short history of the clarinet. Heinrich Joseph Baermann (1784-1847), Carl's father, was a renowned virtuoso who influenced many composers to write for the clarinet. Carl Maria Von Weber and Felix Mendelssohn dedicated the majority of their clarinet compositions to him.

Although Carl, his son, was responsible for many new keys and improvements on the crude clarinet of his day, he is best remembered for his method book. After concertizing with his father all over Europe, Carl finally succeeded him as principal clarinetist in the Munich Court Orchestra.

"Etude No. 3" is taken from Carl Baermann's Twenty-four Etudes for Clarinet with piano accompaniment. It is an extremely lyrical solo, utilizing simple, but interesting rhythms. It's style and form are characteristic of the Romantic period (nineteenth century) in music history. The music of this period was free, impulsive, and individual in nature.

Measure 1-4   The dotted eighth-sixteenth note rhythm is new to you. The dotted eighth is equal to three tied sixteenth notes and it is customary to put a slight space after the dotted eighth note. Think of the third sixteenth note of a beat as a rest instead of a note. A sixteenth rest looks like this ⅞ and is equal to 1/4 of a beat. In the exercise below the first two measures show the rhythm of this figure as it should sound. The rest of the exercise is notated as a dotted eighth and sixteenth note. If a song is slower and more lyrical, the dotted eighth note should not be played quite as short.

PREPARATION 5

One way to help you play more lyrically is to keep your right hand fingers down whenever possible. The right hand can be kept down on any notes between the throat tones of "G" to "B♭". This lessens the movement of the right hand which can be too abrupt and cause squeaks and rough spots. By keeping your right hand down these tones will also be more resonant. In this solo you can use this technique in the first four measures and many other places later.

Try the following example, keeping your right hand down. Be sure to start slowly and evenly and gradually increase the speed.

PREPARATION 6

Keep the right hand down_____

In the solo, the first two measures should lead or drive to the first note ("E") of measure 3, which is the peak of the first four-bar phrase.

Measure 5-8   The long "B" often has a fuzzy or airy sound. To improve the quality of this note, keep the throat open, as if you were yawning. Imagine the sound is reaching or projecting to the back of the room, no matter what dynamic level you are playing. Legato tongue marks (staccatos with a slur) as in measure 6 should be played with no break between the notes, but with a definite stroke of the tongue. It may help to think of the syllable "da" instead of "ta". Crescendo in measure 6, especially on the "B", so the sound will move forward to the first note of the next measure. This will also help connect the two notes, even though the "G" is to be tongued. In measure 8 it is best to play the "B" with the left little finger and the "C♯" with the right little finger. This will help make the movement from "C♯" to "E" smoother.

Measure 9-13   In the next three measures play the sixteenth note for its full value before tonguing the quarter note on the third beat. Instead of ending another four-measure phrase in measure 12, lead into measure 13 by swelling the sound throughout the measure.

Measure 14-16   Measure 15 is the peak of the first sixteen measures. Build the dynamic level in the two measures preceding so measure 15 will not be suddenly too loud. Hold the high "C" on the third beat for its full value and perhaps a little longer for emphasis.

Measure 17-20   This four-measure phrase should be played as measures 13-16, starting softly with a gradual crescendo. Prepare for the "G" at the beginning of measure 17 so it doesn't explode. Take a quick, big breath at the end of measure 16, think of the pitch of the note, and set your embouchure. There is very little time to do this, but as you become more experienced this will be an automatic response. In measure 20 use a slight ritard to heighten the feeling of the con moto starting in measure 21.

Measure 21-24   This section, "con moto", should be played slightly faster. Now the dotted eighth notes should be a little shorter. In measures 21 and 22 there is a small note with a slash before the fourth beat. These are called grace notes. These notes embellish or decorate the notes on the beat. Play each grace note just ahead of the beat, then play the regular notes on the beat. Try using the right little finger for "B" and the left little finger for the "C" in this section. You can hold the left little finger down for the "B". These fingerings will keep the movement from "B" to "G" all in the right hand. Watch the dynamic markings carefully and crescendo on the last two beats of measures 21 and 22.

Measure 25-32   Use a full, rich tone in the chalameau register, low "E" to the throat tone "B♭". This will be the first spot in this solo that is that low, so bring it out. Whenever there is a large skip in the melody as at the end of measure 26, crescendo slightly on the note preceding the skip. This will help the notes sound more connected even when they are tongued. Use this technique again on the "E" to "D" skip in measure 27 and give the "D" a little extra time since it is the climax of this phrase. Be sure to keep the sound full at measure 28 so you'll be able to decrescendo more in the following measures. With the ritard in measure 31 play the last eighth note of the measure slightly longer. There is no piano part on the first beat of measure 32, so the accompanist takes the beat from the soloist.

A good warm-up to use each day is a three-measure decrescendo as shown below. Start with the air stream full and steady and gradually decrescendo to pianissimo (very soft).

PREPARATION 7

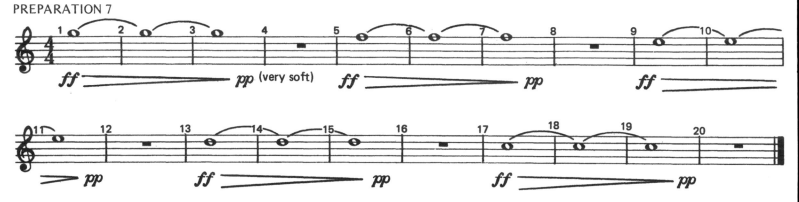

It will help if you remember that very little diaphragm support is needed when playing fortissimo. However, as the tone diminishes, more and more support is needed, until at pianissimo very little air is used but a maximum amount of support is demanded. Make sure the pitch of each note stays the same from fortissimo to pianissimo and the tone keeps its center or core.

Measure 33-36   The return of Tempo I begins with a restatement of the first melody. Be careful of the differences in articulation, such as in measures 1 and 33. Catch a quick breath at the end of measure 34 rather than at the end of measure 36.

Measure 37-40   These measures should be connected by using a slight crescendo on the last note. Build each of the measures to the "G" on the first beat of measure 39 which is the peak of this phrase. If absolutely necessary, a short breath can be taken after the first beat of measure 40. You can take a big, full breath at the end of measure 40 and even take a little extra time. Be sure your accompanist is aware that you'll be taking a little time so you both can re-enter at measure 41 together.

Measure 41-44   This starts a new phrase structured around the interval of a major sixth. Make these skips very smooth and gradually crescendo to the high "D" in measure 44. Since the note immediately preceding this high "D" is the same note, be sure to tongue the first note of measure 44 and give it a little extra length for emphasis. Keep your right hand down through the "G" in measure 45 to help make the line smoother.

Measure 45-52   Decrescendo each five-note motive from measure 45 to measure 51. The low "F♯" in measure 49 should be played with the right little finger.

Your accompanist will control the ritard in measure 51. You both should "breath" at the end of measure 51 so the attack is together in measure 52. Keep the center in the tone even though it is played pianissimo. The pitch could go sharp since it is so soft, so think of keeping it low by taking a little less mouthpiece in your mouth or relaxing the embouchure slightly. You should cue the release of the last note by making a small up and down motion with the bell of your instrument.

Etude No. 3

Carl Baermann
(1811-1885)

Gavotte

musical terms

tranquillo   **tranquil, quiet**
la seconda volta   **the second time**

new note

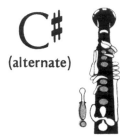

C♯
(alternate)

Johann Sebastian Bach (1685-1750) is recognized as one of the greatest composers in all music history and his compositional excellence represents the heighth of music in the Baroque period.

The suite and the partita had their origins in dances and the contrasts within the set were well established by Bach. The order of movements found in his suites is: allemande, courante, sarabande, intermezzi and gigue. The intermezzi included many optional dances such as bourrees, gavottes, passepieds, polonaises, rigaudon, anglaise, loures, airs, or minuets and were used at the composers discretion.

In this suite Bach used the gavotte as his optional dance. The gavotte is usually a moderate four-four movement with an upbeat of two quarter notes and phrases beginning and ending in the middle of measures. The character of the dance should be graceful and elegant, though not too slow.

Since the clarinet was not invented until around 1700 by J.C. Denner of Nuremberg, very little music can be found written for the instrument until about the middle of the eighteenth century. Therefore, the clarinetist isn't able to play Baroque music unless he uses transcriptions, special arrangements for the clarinet. This suite is the last of a group of six written for the harpsichord titled English Suites. The original, in the key of D major, is extremely thin in texture with a single melodic line in each of the two voices, both written in the treble clef. The left hand moving eighth notes were retained and an extra harmony part was constructed for the right hand accompaniment part. Notice the constant reiteration of the tonic ("C") in the left hand of the accompaniment. Dance pieces with long drones, the repetition of the tonic, were often called "musettes" after a French bagpipe of the 17th and 18th century.

Measure 1-4   Even though this piece should be played in a quiet, pastoral style, be sure to start mezzo forte on the first time. A solo with exact repeats such as this one is usually played with different dynamic levels for contrast so the repeat should be played piano. The entire solo is played legato indicated by the phrase mark above each group of measures. Use the legato tongue, the syllable "da" for each note.

In the first full measure there is a new figure called a mordent, indicated by the mark ∿. A mordent is an embellishment of two or more notes played before the written note. This particular mordent uses the principle (written) note and the nearest upper scale note with an accent on the first note of the group. Since the tempo in this gavotte is moderate, the mordent should contain from four to six notes and should start on the upper scale note. The illustration shows how the mordent looks, written out. A group of four notes will come on the first half of beat 1 and the remaining two notes on the last half of the beat. Practice the exercise below with the metronome set slowly at first. This exercise divides the beat into two, three, four, six, and eight equal parts. Try to make each measure smooth and even.

ILLUSTRATION 1

PREPARATION 8

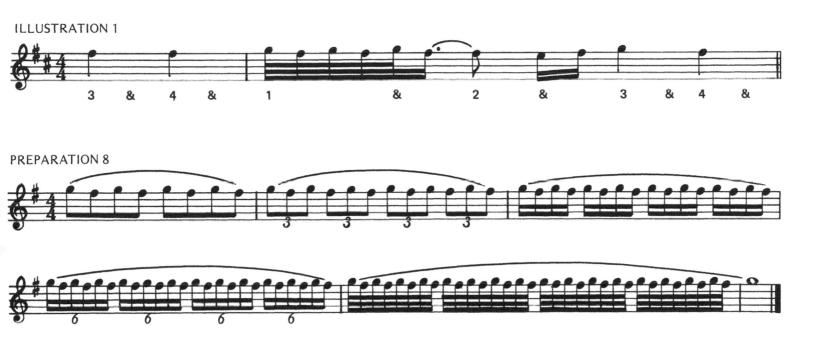

Use the right little finger for the "C♯" in measure 3 and all other "C♯'s" in this solo. This will keep the finger movement to a minimum. You may also want to keep the right hand down from the "D" to "A" and back to "F" in measure 4.

Measure 5-8   This begins the second phrase which is slightly extended. Crescendo to the high "B" in measure 6. By using this crescendo and thinking of the pitch before you play it, the sound will not "explode". Keep the right hand down for the rest of the phrase and be sure to decrescendo to finish off the phrase.

Measure 9-16   Here the main theme is restated, this time a minor third higher. The mordent is played as it was in measures 1 and 5. You may want to try the exercise shown above starting on the two notes of this mordent. Starting the phrase in measure 11 "piano" makes a pleasant contrast in the solo. This will give you a wider range of dynamics to use especially in building the crescendo to the peak in measure 16.

Measure 17-26 Beginning at measure 17, the main theme returns. Use the same ideas and techniques as in the beginning. Keep the rhythm steady and the eighth notes very precise. On the repeat use a softer dynamic level and a slight ritard at the end. You should indicate the release on the last note with a slight up-down motion with the bell of your instrument.

Gavotte

Johann Sebastian Bach
(1685-1750)

Spring Time

musical terms

allegretto	**light and cheerful, a little faster than moderato**
piu mosso	**a little more motion, a little faster**
a tempo	**in tempo, in time, return to the tempo preceding a rit.**
dolce	**sweetly**

Louis Stanislaw Xaver Verroust, a French oboist, teacher and composer, lived during the Romantic period of music history. He is probably best remembered for his oboe method. Verroust, like so many Romantic composers, is a realist. They believed music could tell a story, imitate sounds of nature, and express visual scenes. In this solo Spring is the theme.

"Spring Time" must be played very legato, as smoothly connected as possible. To help get the feel of playing legato, practice the following exercise. The breath support should remain constant and the embouchure changed only slightly. The important thing is to make the notes equal and connected. At first you may have to take a breath after each measure. Then try to do as many measures as you can on one breath. Start with the metronome set at ♩ =60, later increase the speed.

PREPARATION 9

Measure 1-6   The pianist sets the tempo for the solo. He should play with a full sound gradually diminishing to allow the soloist to enter at "*mp*" and be heard.

One characteristic of Romantic music is the use of wide ranges of expression. Although there are crescendos and decrescendos within every one or two measures, the overall phrase is four measures in length and one overall crescendo and decrescendo should be felt in that four measures.

Whenever there are two slurred eighth notes, make them equal in length and with a slight emphasis on the first note of each slur. Try to put a small decrescendo on each group of two notes. This will help you keep the notes from sounding too short or chopped.

Measure 7-10   Watch the articulation carefully. In measure 8 the notes are slurred starting on the beat. In measure 9 the beginning of the slur is on the "and" of the beat. The same techniques of accenting the first note and putting a slight decrescendo on each group should be used. Check your clarinet for tuning of particular notes. If the high "D" that occurs in measure 10 is sharp, leave off the right little finger and check to see if that lowers the pitch slightly. Be sure to slur all five notes of measure 10. To help connect the high "D" to the "D" on the third beat, "pop" your left hand first finger down quickly.

Measure 11-14   Here the tempo should be increased slightly, "poco piu mosso". You should also play with a little more sound than at the beginning. Again "round off" the last notes of the slurs, so the notes don't sound chopped. When you have large skips keep the air stream steady and well supported. Remember that a slight crescendo and some intensity as the skips go up will help connect the notes smoothly.

Also keep your fingers and embouchure relaxed. Practice the following interval exercises with the thought of connecting the two notes.

PREPARATION 10

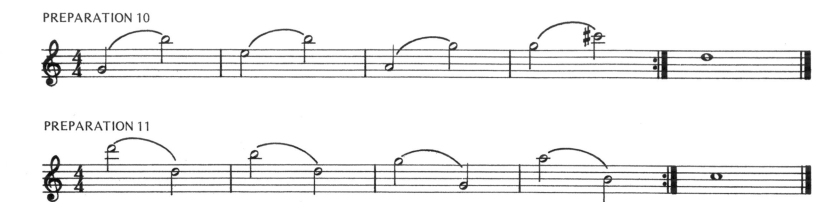

PREPARATION 11

Measure 15-18   When playing the "B-A♯-B" movement, keep the right hand down to help smoothness and resonance. You can keep the right hand down for the entire measure if it will help. Measure 18 is the end of the "piu mosso" movement so put a slight pause after the third beat. Be sure your accompanist is aware of what you are doing and watches you for the pick-up notes. With these pick-up notes the solo returns to the original tempo.

Measure 19-22   The opening theme returns at measure 19 with the same articulation for the first four measures. Use the same techniques here that were discussed earlier.

Measure 23-26   Beginning in this measure the melody and articulations are varied slightly. Be sure to tongue the beginning of each group of slurred notes and round off the last notes of the group to make the solo more musical. Build up to measure 25, the climax of the solo. The first "B" in the measure should be played with a slight tenuto and forte for emphasis. On the first time through the "poco rit." and "Fine" should not be played.

Measure 27-36   While the accompanist plays the eight measure interlude, draw any moisture out of your mouthpiece as quietly as possible. In measure 33 and 34 begin preparing for the three pick-up notes. Since they are "A's" followed by a "D" keep the right-hand down. Be sure to tongue these notes with a legato tongue.

Measure 37-42   Remember the right little finger is not used for high "C♯". This makes the note higher in pitch. To make the note speak easier, roll the first finger of the left hand down on the rim of the key instead of lifting it off the key. Use the right little finger for "B" in measure 40 and for "C♯" in measure 41. Return to the beginning to complete the solo. For contrast take a little longer to play the eighth note pick-ups with tenuto marks.

Measure 25-26   Remember to gradually slow down in these measures since it is the second time through the solo.

Spring Time

Louis Verroust
(1814-1863)

Siciliano and Minuet

new notes

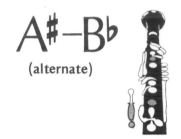

A#−B♭

(alternate)

Bach uses this "Siciliano" in his E♭ Major Flute Sonata as a slow movement between two faster movements. The siciliano was used by many seventeenth and eighteenth century composers to depict soft rural and pastoral scenes. Originally a dance of Sicilian peasants, a siciliano is usually found in 6/8 or 12/8 time and is graceful, slow and soothing in character. Although in many recordings made by flutists a wide range of tempos (from 100 to 120) can be found, the movement will sound more natural and graceful in a moderate tempo. Set the metronome at around ♪=104 and count six eighth notes for each measure.

Upon investigation of this "Siliciano" in a volume of Bach's complete works, the student may be surprised to learn that Bach gave no indication of tempo, dynamics, or articulation. It was customary in the Baroque and Classical eras for the composer to leave out any interpretive markings, knowing that the individual performer would decide upon his own interpretation. Traditions became accepted through the years so certain works are now performed in particular ways. It would seem very non-musical to play the piece today as Bach wrote it, without any markings whatsoever.

Before the soloist gives the downbeat, the tempo should be well-established in the minds of both performers. This can be easily done by indicating six eighth notes to the accompanist with the bell of the clarinet.

Measure 1-4   The dotted eighth-sixteenth note figure appears throughout the solo. Because the continuous sixteenth note pattern occurs in the accompaniment, the figure must be very precise. Practice the following exercise with the metronome set at ♪=208. Since this is the first four measures of the solo you may also want to try it with your accompanist.

PREPARATION 12

Since the "Siciliano" is graceful and lyrical, use a legato tongue to connect the eighth notes on beats 3 and 4 of the first measure and any other similar places. This will help the notes sound, without exploding. If you need a breath, you could take one at the end of measure 2, but it would sound better if you could play the entire phrase, four measures, on one breath. Stay relaxed when moving to the high "B" in measure 3. In measure 4 you'll see a small-size eighth note. This is called an appoggiatura, Italian for "lean on". In Baroque music if this note precedes a dotted note, it takes two thirds of that note's value. Measure 4 should be played as shown below.

ILLUSTRATION 2

WRITTEN   PLAYED

Measure 5-9   This entire measure moves or drives to the first note of measure 6. Prepare for the high "D" so it doesn't explode or sound out of context with the other notes. Remember, in playing large intervals, the breath support must be maintained. The first two notes of measure 6 end another musical passage. Be sure to press the first note and decrescendo into the second note ♩♩. This is done by using less air and more breath support. Be careful that the pitch does not change. Follow the melodic line for the natural crescendo - decrescendo.

Measure 10-22 You'll probably need to take a breath at the end of measure 11 since this phrase is a little longer. In measure 12 try rolling your first finger left hand down when moving from the "F" to "D". This should help this note speak easier than lifting the finger abruptly. Drive this phrase through to the first note of measure 14 but be sure to keep the sixteenth notes rhythmically in unison with the accompaniment.

In measures 17 and 18, try using the new "one and two" fingering for "A♯". This makes the transition from "F♯" much smoother, since the change is made by lifting only the second and third fingers of the left hand. This fingering makes the pitch of the note higher which in this case is desirable because it acts as a leading tone into the "B" that follows. If you need a breath in measure 18, take a quick one through the corners of the mouth, keeping the embouchure intact as much as possible. Hold the "D♯" as long as possible before taking your breath so it will not sound "chopped off". Use the right little finger for the first note ("B") in measure 20 and keep your right hand down for the throat tones until you get to "G". Put a little more accent on the "G" in measure 21.

Measure 23-28 In measures 27 and 28 use the left little finger on "B" in preparation for the "D♯" which must be played with the right little finger. You could take a breath in measure 27, but it would be better to wait until measure 28. From measure 26 to the end use resonant fingerings wherever possible for clarity and smoothness.

Measure 29-30 The phrase beginning with the pick-up to measure 29 should drive to the fourth beat of measure 30. In this case the rhythmic figure and appoggiatura should be played precisely with the piano. The example below will show how this fits into the measure. The figure on beat 4 is a dotted sixteenth-thirty-second. A thirty-second is equal to ¼ of the beat in this case. As shown it should come right after the "and" of beat 4.

ILLUSTRATION 3

When the appoggiatura precedes a note that can be divided into two parts, it assumes half of the value of that note, so this appoggiatura should be played as two eighth notes.

Measure 31-33 Be very careful that these eighth notes are precise and not hurried. Measure 32 should be broken down into six beats for study. Since the solo and accompaniment both have the trill, they must be together. The examples below show you the written notation and the notes that should be played.

ILLUSTRATION 4

You may want to review trilling with the following exercise. Set the metronome at ♩=60 and practice for smoothness and precision. Choose whichever "C" fingering is easier for you to trill.

PREPARATION 13

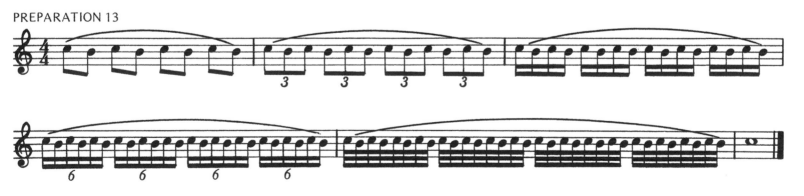

Be sure to ritard beginning in measure 32 and lead your accompanist into measure 33 by giving a cue on the downbeat of the measure.

G (trill)

A#–Bb (alternate)

The "Minuet", the second dance of this set, was another optional dance used by composers. This was one of the intermezzi dances before the final movement of Bach's <u>Suite No. 2 in B minor</u> for flute and has been transposed up one-half step to the key of C minor.

The minuet is a dance in three-four meter and moderately slow. It should be played in a stately but graceful and elegant manner. The phrases in this dance are defined by the dynamics rather than the melodic structure.

Measure 1-4   The first phrase should be played in a rather broad legato style at about a forte. In measure 2 another appoggiatura occurs which takes two thirds of the note it precedes. The example below will show you the written notation and performance notation.

ILLUSTRATION 5

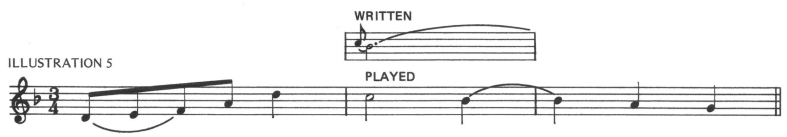

Many of the long tones in this solo are throat tones. Try to use resonant fingerings whenever possible to help make these clear. In measure 3 of the accompaniment the appoggiatura takes one-half of the note it precedes, so the bass line should be played as three quarter notes. The quarter note trill in the solo should be approached from the scale note above the written note. This measure would look like this if written out.

ILLUSTRATION 6

You should practice the exercise below so the trill is precise. Set the metronome at ♩=60 to begin. Later you can increase the tempo to the marked tempo of the solo. The "F-G" trill may be easier to play if you'll use an alternate fingering. Keep the thumb down for "F" and add the left hand "G#-Ab" key to trill "G".

PREPARATION 14

Measure 5-8   This phrase should be played in direct contrast — with a light, delicate staccato. Try playing the "Bb" in this measure with an alternate fingering using the "A" key and the second side key from the top on the right. Practice using this fingering in the exercise below.

PREPARATION 15

The appoggiatura in measure 8 goes by the two-thirds rule so the "F" should be a half note and the "E" a quarter note. Remember to repeat the first eight measures.

Measure 9-12   The third section begins here, again forte and legato. By now you can figure out how the appoggiaturas should be played in the remainder of the solo. On all, slightly accent the first note, which appears as the small note.

Measure 13-15 Another light, staccato section begins here. The trill in this phrase falls on a low "A" and "G", so practice the trill exercise using these notes.

Measure 16-24 The final two sections should not present any problems. Be sure to use the resonant fingerings on the sustained throat tones, "Bb" and "A". The appoggiatura in measure 23 should be played as two eighth notes with a slight emphasis on the first note. Remember to go back to measure 9 for the repeat. Generally a slight ritard is played on the repeat at the end.

MASTER SOLOS
INTERMEDIATE
LEVEL
**Edited & Performed
by Ramon Kireilis**

Clarinet

HAL•LEONARD®

Piano (B♭ Clarinet)

Intermediate Level

MASTER SOLOS
by Ramon Kireilis

EDITED by Linda Rutherford

Contents

ISBN 978-0-7935-9548-8

Copyright © 1975 by HAL LEONARD LLC
International Copyright Secured All Rights Reserved

Visit Hal Leonard Online at
www.halleonard.com

Contact Us:
Hal Leonard
7777 West Bluemound Road
Milwaukee, WI 53213
Email: info@halleonard.com

In Europe contact:
Hal Leonard Europe Limited
42 Wigmore Street
Marylebone, London, W1U 2RN
Email: info@halleonardeurope.com

In Australia contact:
Hal Leonard Australia Pty. Ltd.
4 Lentara Court
Cheltenham, Victoria, 3192 Australia
Email: info@halleonard.com.au

Gymnopédie No. 1

Erik Satie
(1866-1925)

pedal simile

4

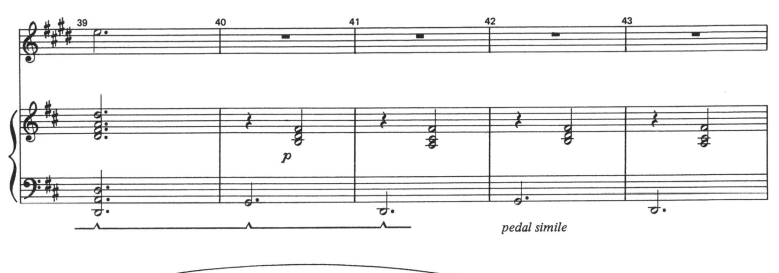

pedal simile

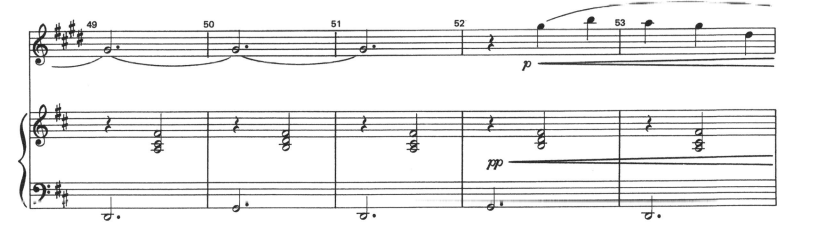

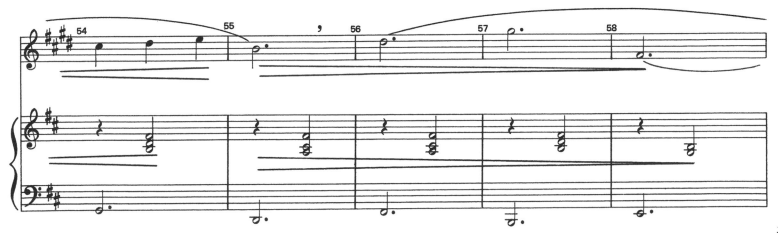

Etude No. 3

Carl Baermann
(1811-1885)

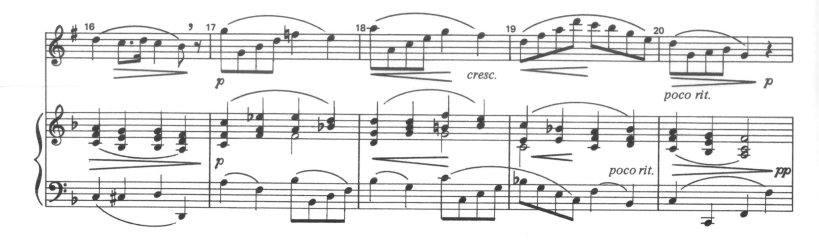

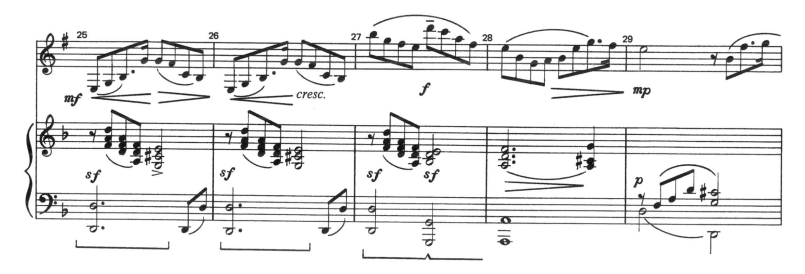

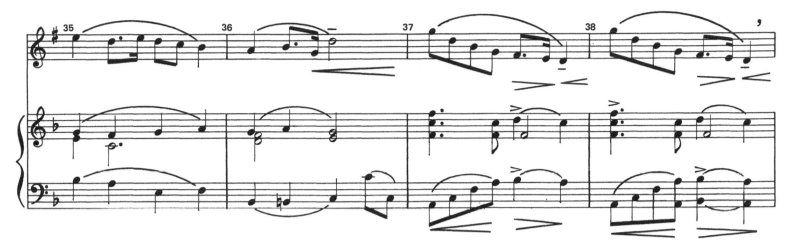

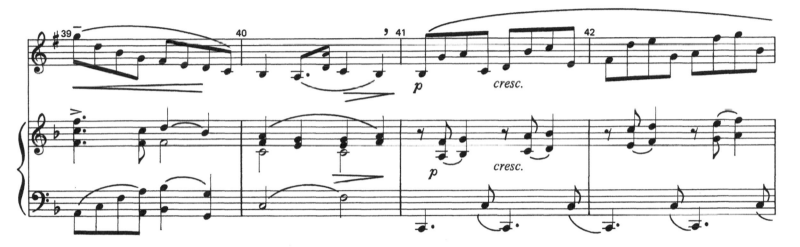

9

Gavotte

Johann Sebastian Bach
(1685-1750)

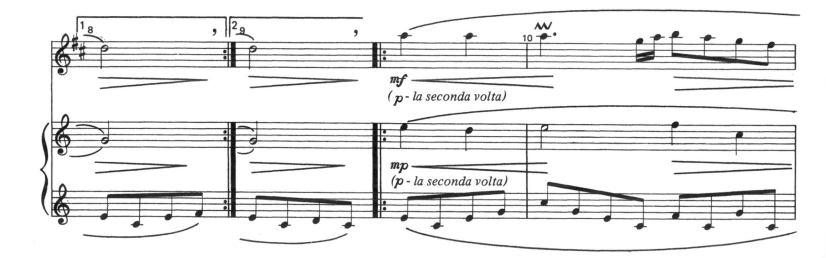

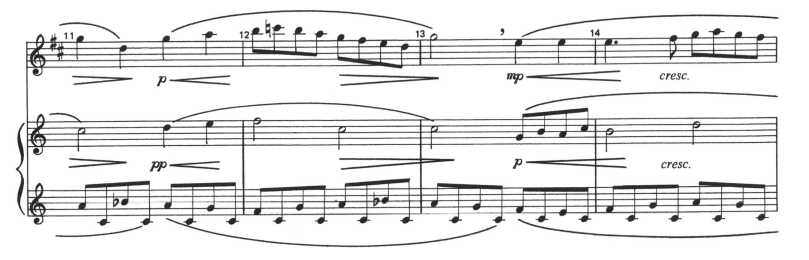

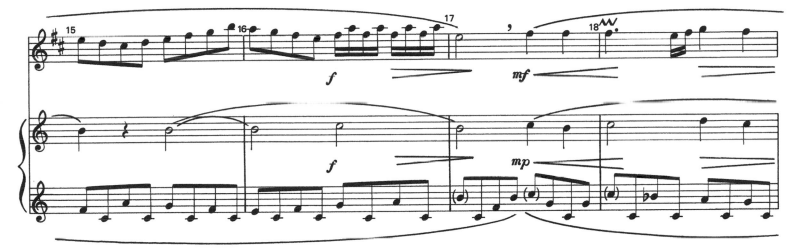

11

Spring Time

Louis Verroust
(1814-1863)

Tempo I

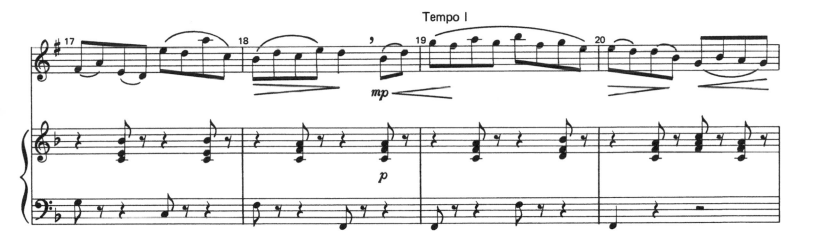

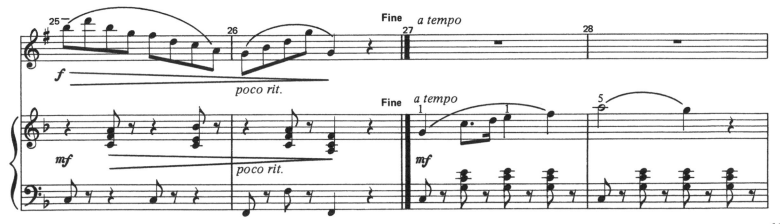

13

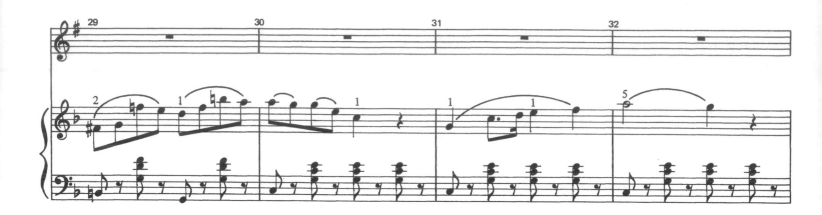

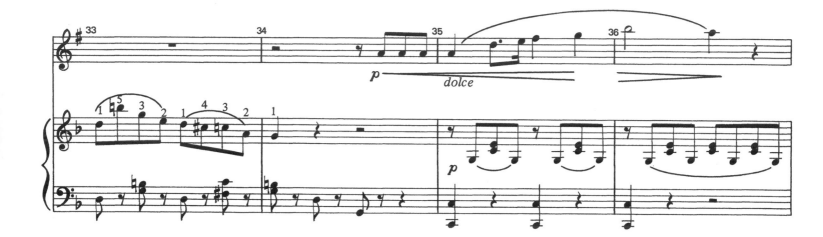

D.S. al Fine

D.S. al Fine

14

Siciliano

Johann Sebastian Bach
(1685-1750)

M.M. ♪ = 100

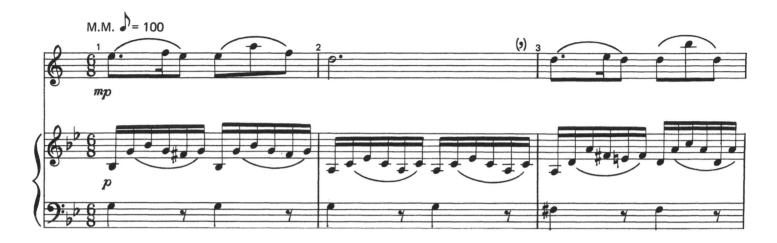

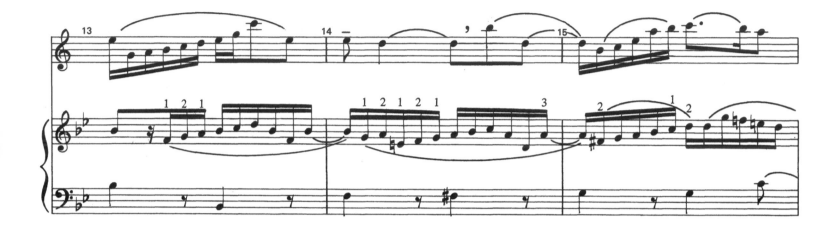

16

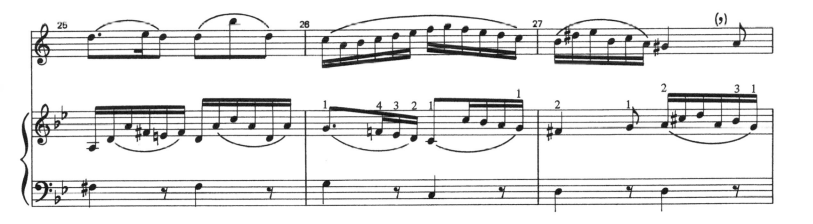

17

Minuet

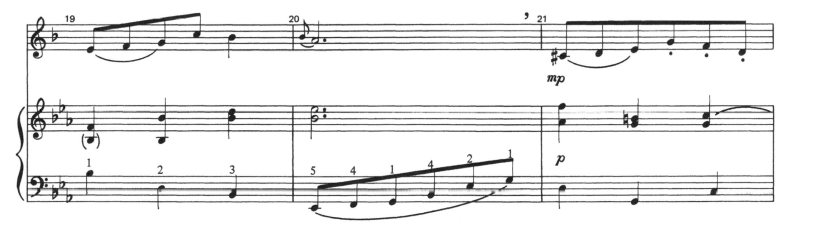

Andante

Alexandre Beon

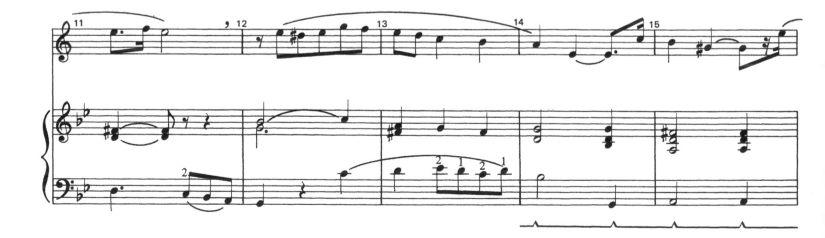

21

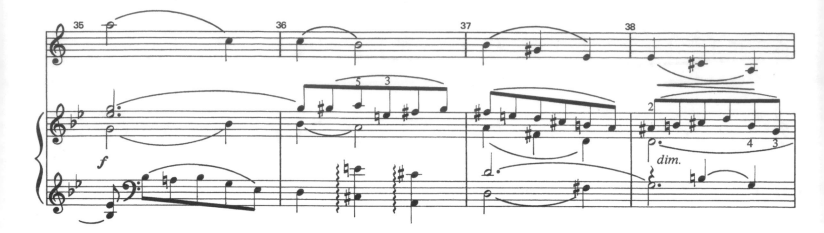

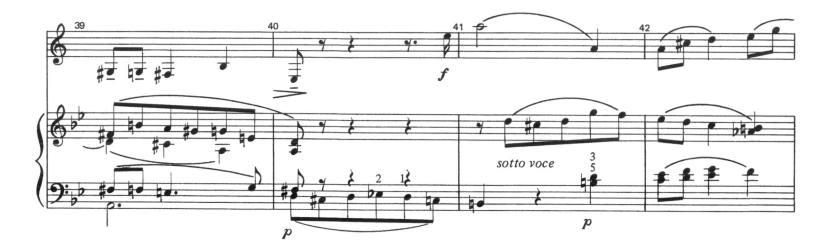

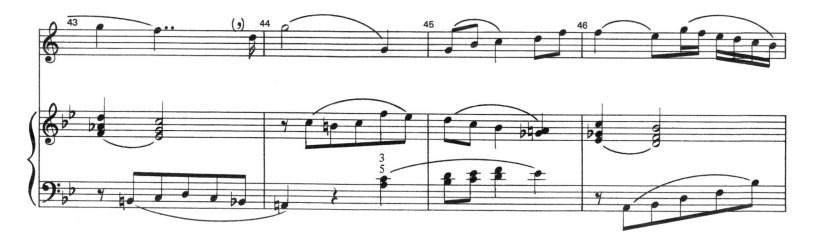

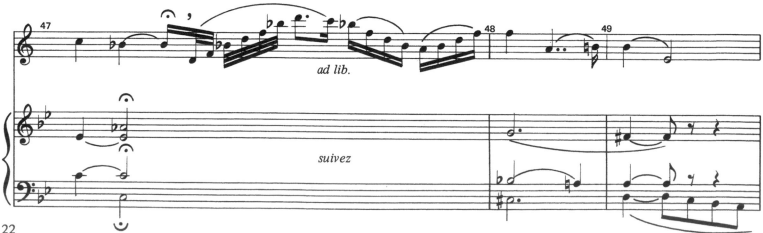

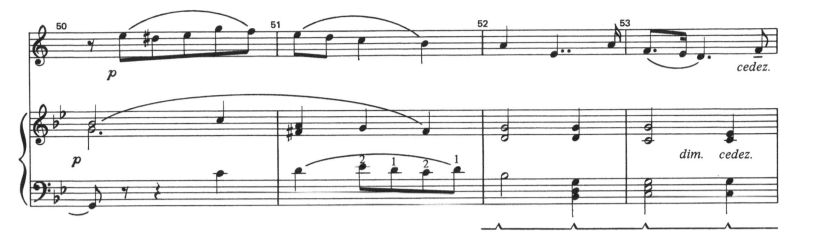

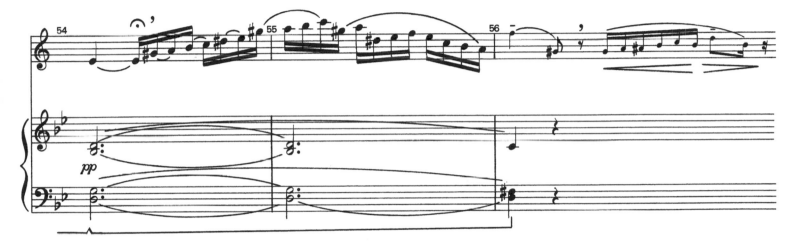

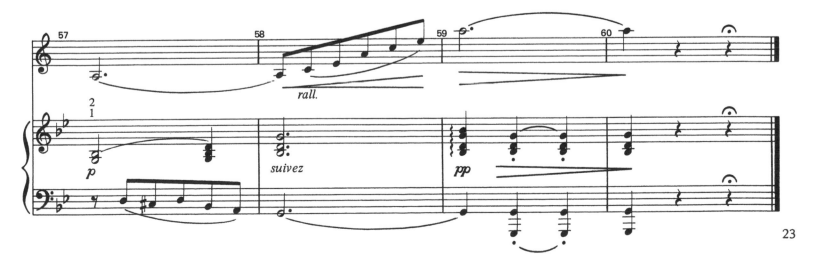

Rondo Allegretto

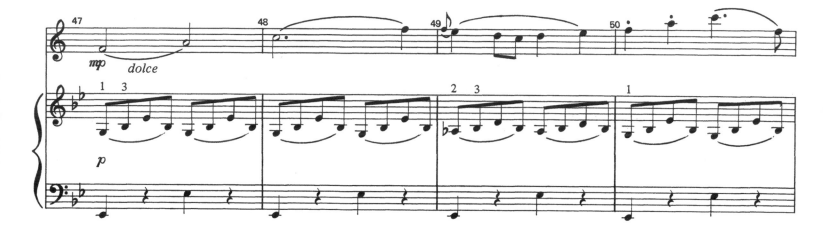

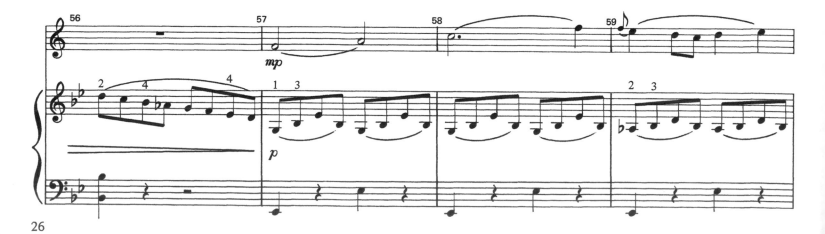

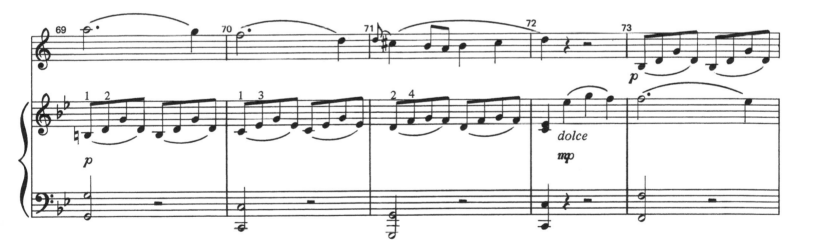

27

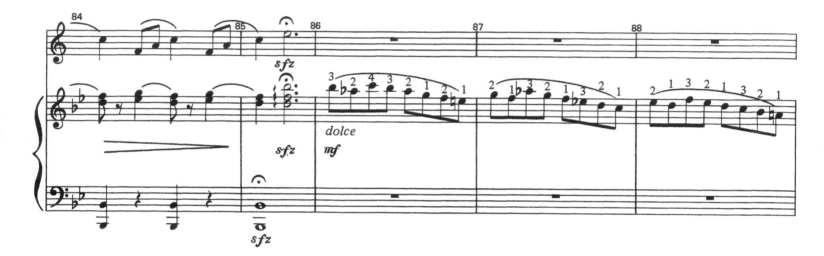

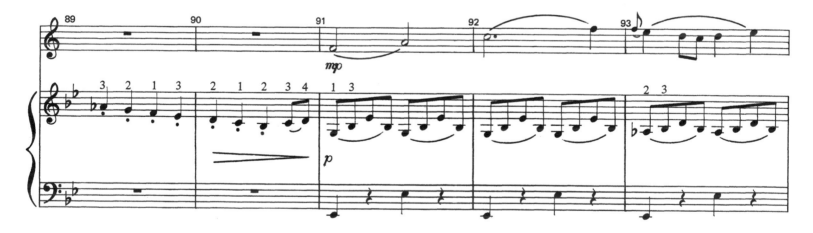

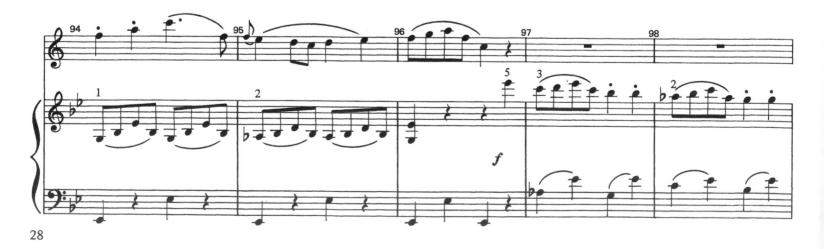

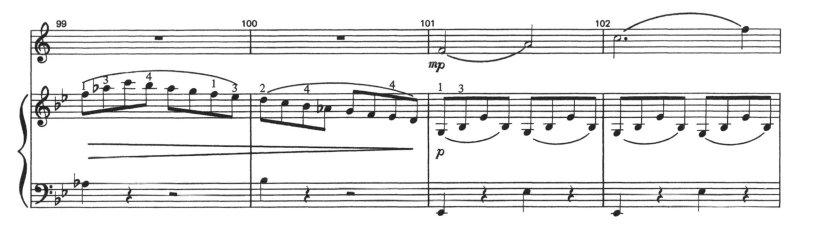

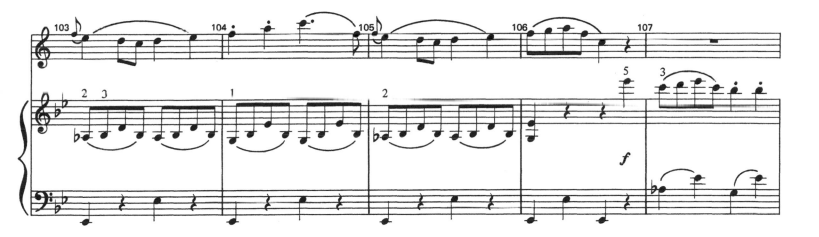

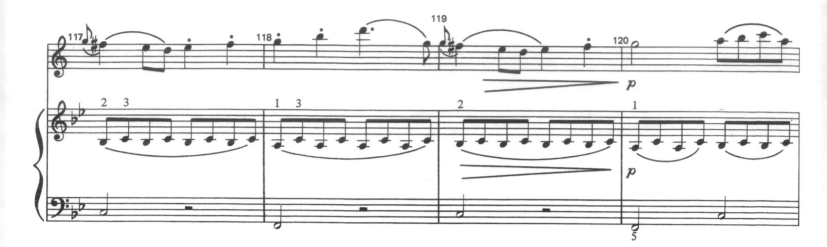

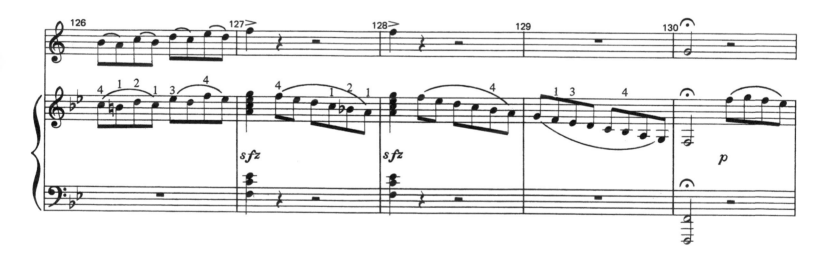

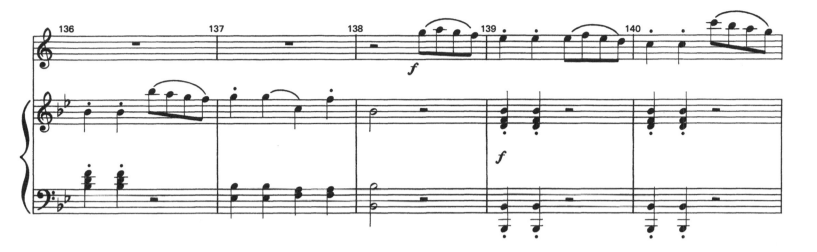

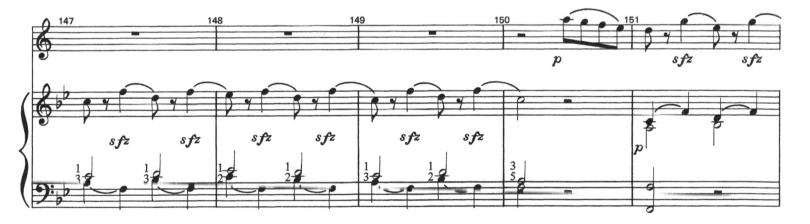

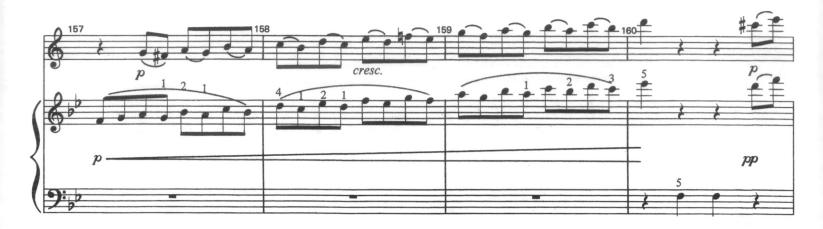

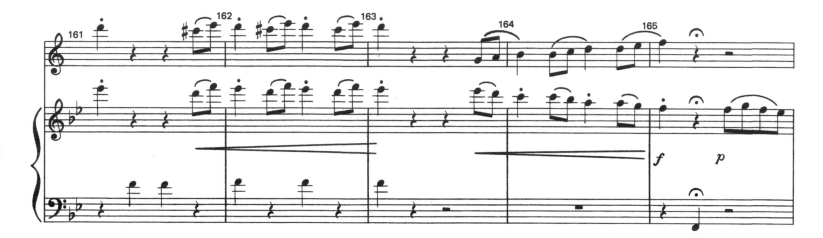

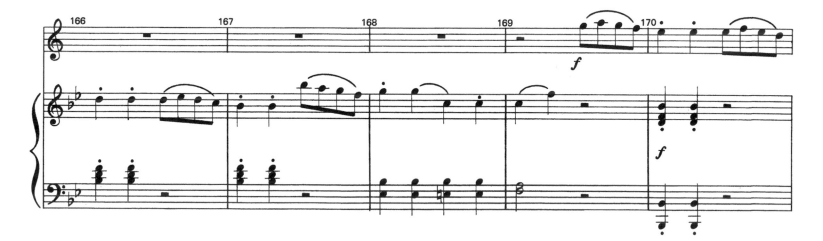

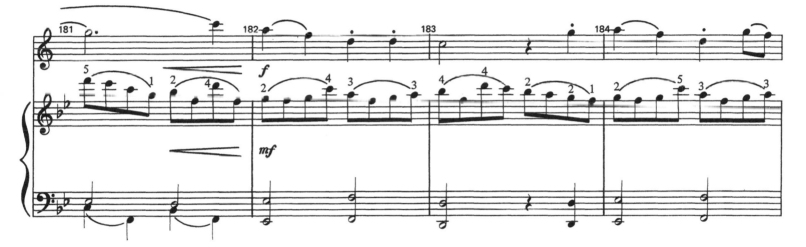

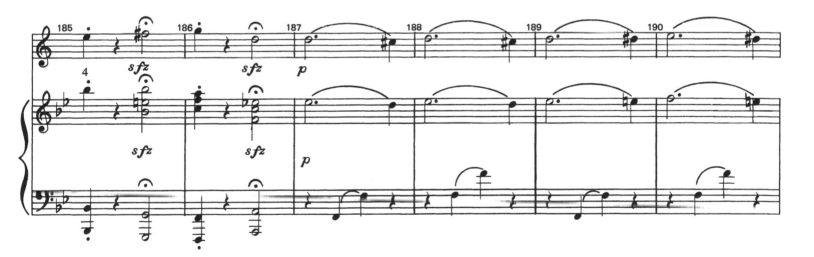

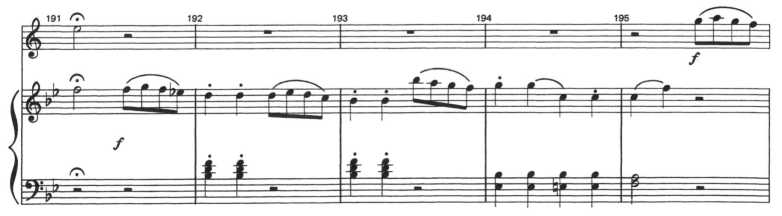

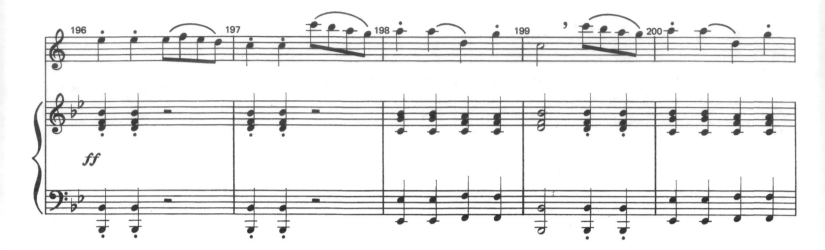

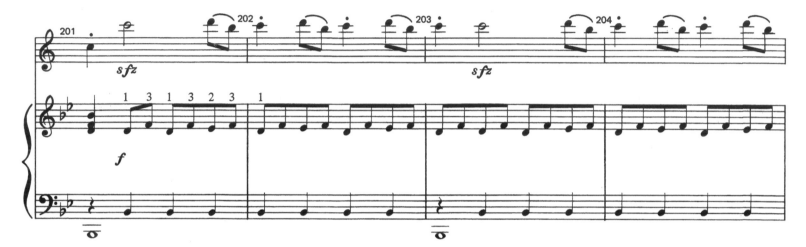

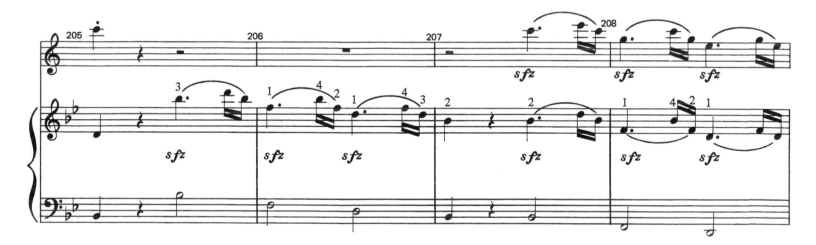

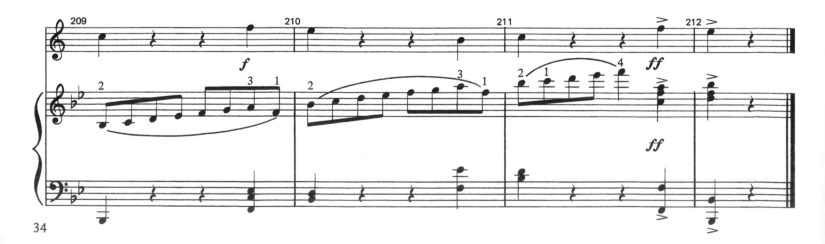

To Ramon Kireilis

Revery

Normand Lockwood
(1906-2002)

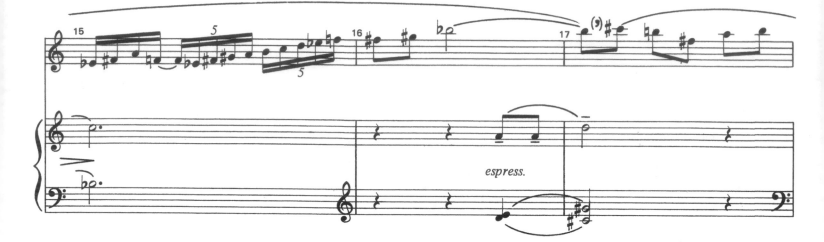

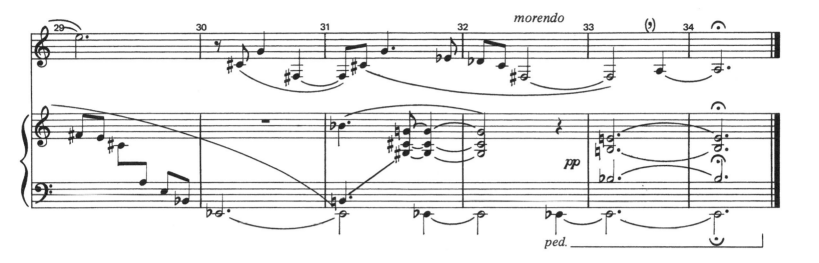

Dance

38

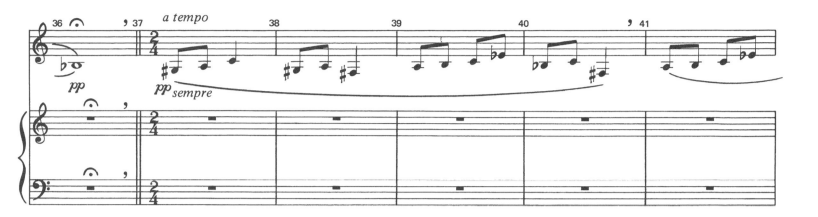

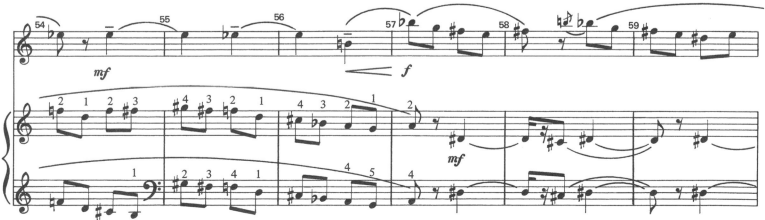

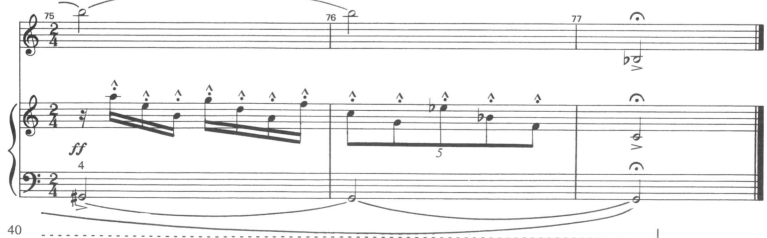

Siciliano

Johann Sebastian Bach
(1685-1750)

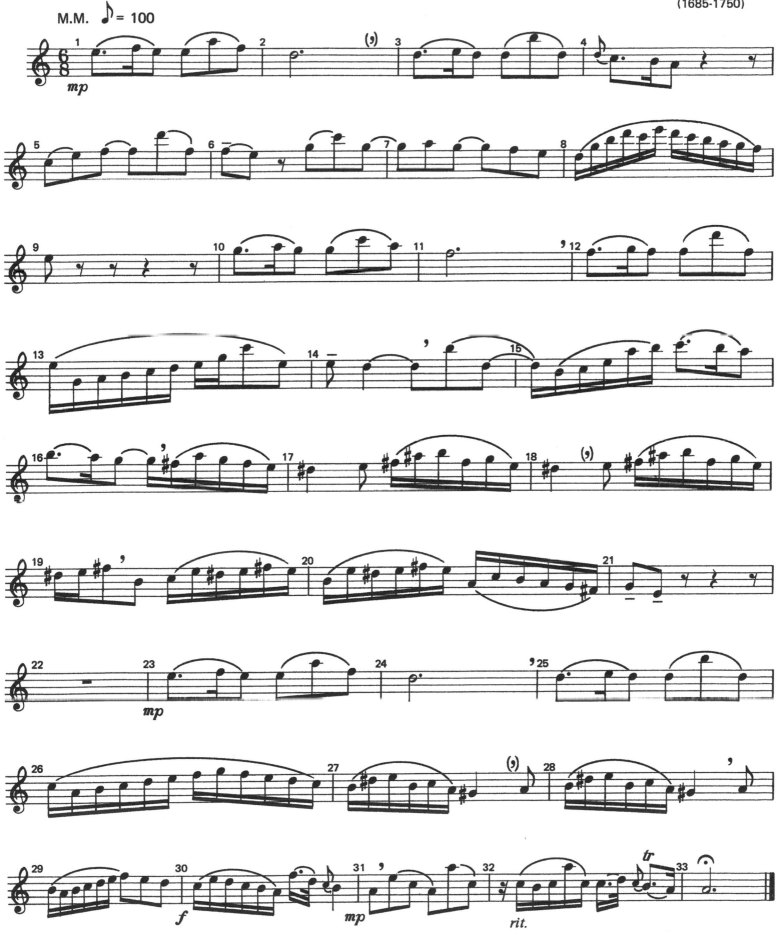

Minuet

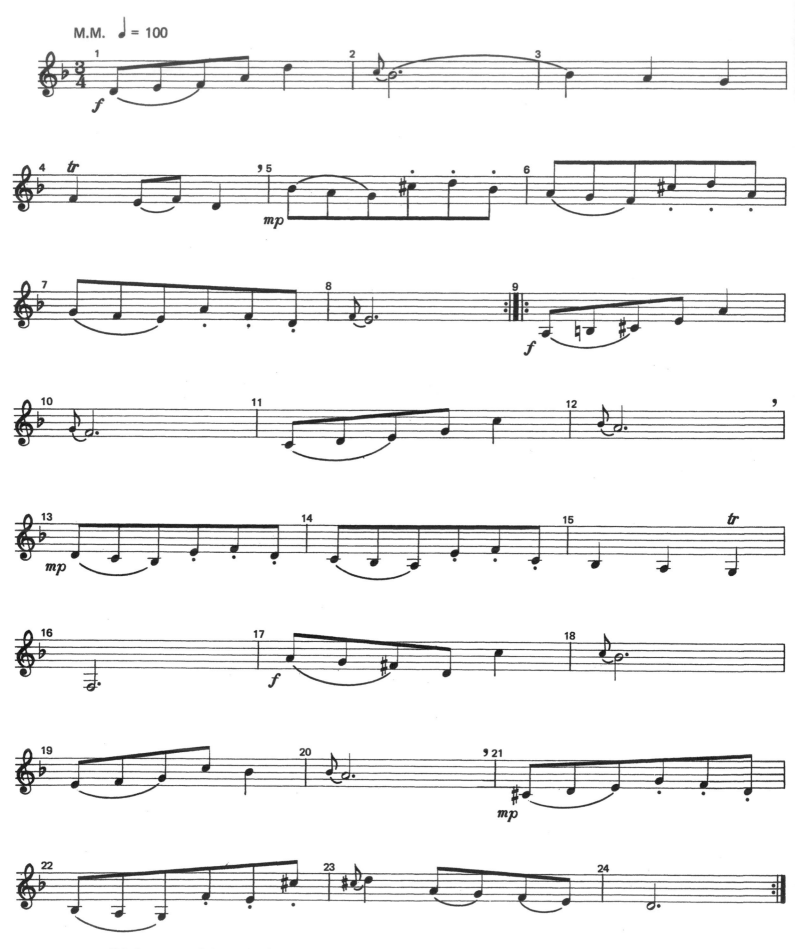

Andante

musical terms

andante	**moderate tempo**
avec charme	**with charm**
rall.	**abbreviation for rallentando meaning gradually slower**
ad lib.	**ad libitum - at will. Interpret passage without a strict tempo.**
cedez	**French meaning "give way", go a little slower or play a note slightly longer**

new notes

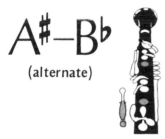

A♯–B♭ (alternate)

Alexandre Beon was a Belgian composer who wrote the majority of his works during the first quarter of this century. His compositions and others are now out-of-print. This is largely due to the death of the older virtuosic school of performance in which compositions demanded great technical skill in their performance; Beon's <u>Concerto</u> embraces this style.

A concerto is usually a three movement composition for a solo instrument and orchestra. This "Andante" is the middle, slower movement of Beon's <u>Concerto</u> arranged for clarinet and piano.

The "Andante" is a beautiful, cantabile (song-like), melodic movement requiring much less technical prowess than the other movements. Here, you should strive for beauty of tone and phrasing while expressing the sense of line, which like many beautiful melodies is so very simple and transparent in construction. The soloist should imitate singing in this solo, using judicious taste in tempo and phrasing.

"Andante", in this solo, refers to the tempo. The composer offers no other mention of the rate of speed at which the solo is to be played, so allows the soloist a certain amount of freedom. The tempo could fluctuate from ♩=84 to ♩=96, depending on the soloist.

Measure 1-11   Since the accompaniment sets the mood for the entire solo, the soloist should listen to the accompaniment while watching the score to thoroughly understand the solo as a total composition. This study provides the soloist with a sense of confidence. For example, each time the soloist enters with an eighth rest followed by several eighth notes (the main theme), it is preceded by a recognizable descending line of three eighth notes in the bass, usually ending on the key-note ("G"). These will help you feel the rhythm of the eighth notes in preparation for your entrance. To also help you, small notes on the solo part indicate the accompaniment rhythm. The term "avec charme" is a French term meaning "with charm" and not too fast.

In measures 8 and 9 make a difference between the dotted eighth-sixteenth note pattern and the eighth notes. The breath mark is one indication that the first six measures are one phrase and should be played on one breath.

Measure 12-17   This phrase should also be played on one breath; do not breath on the sixteenth rest in measure 15. The last note of measure 16 should be played with the right little finger, moving smoothly into the half note in measure 17. Be sure to hold the note for its full value.

Measure 18-26   Crescendo in measures 18 and 19 so they lead toward the first note of measure 20. Accent the "C♯" slightly and decrescendo the "D" to complete the phrase. The same principles apply to the tenuto mark on the "B" in measure 23, so give this note a little special emphasis. In this phrase double dotted notes are first used. The double dotted quarter note would be equal to 1¾ beat. Practice the exercise on the following page to get the feel of this subdivision. In the first three measures the rhythm is shown through the use of tied notes. Beginning in the fifth measure, dotted notation is used.

PREPARATION 16

Gradually slow down in measure 25 to end the phrase. Use resonant fingerings on the "Bb" and "A" in measures 24 and 25. Try different combinations to give the clearest tone and best in tune.

Measure 27-32   Return to the regular tempo in this measure. Be very careful to make a distinction between the eighth notes, dotted eighth-sixteenth notes, and the double dotted quarter notes. To separate the "A's" at the end of measure 31 and the beginning of measure 32, use legato tonguing.

Measure 32-40   Beginning in this measure the clarinetist takes on the role of accompanist. The piano part has the established melodic figure starting in measure 32. Be sure you play soft enough for the piano to be heard. Play the two "C's" in measure 33 separated but for their full value. The solo and accompaniment are in unison on the first beat of measure 35. Listen and adjust the pitch slightly with your embouchure. You may also want to use this "A" as a tuning note before you begin playing the solo. In measures 39 and 40 keep all the fingerings in the right hand for extra smoothness.

Measure 40-47   During the rests in measure 40, think of the sixteenth note rhythm. The "E" is the last sixteenth note of beat 3. Prepare for this entrance so it will be precisely in time. This phrase begins the only section of the solo that is forte. Play with a full, rich sound and keep your embouchure firm. The louder you play on clarinet, the easier it is for the pitch to go flat. The "C#" in measure 42 will be easier to play with the right little finger. If needed, take a quick breath in measure 43, through the corners of your mouth. This has to last until the "Bb" in measure 47.

Measure 47-49   In measures 47 and 56 there are two ad lib sections. "Ad lib" means "at will" so the soloist takes the written notation and "bends" the rhythm to give the phrase inflection. When you are first learning these measures, it will be easier if you divide it into beats and practice it with the metronome. The accompanist has a half note with a fermata and listens to the solo part to enter on the next chord accurately. "Suivez" in the accompaniment means "with the part", listening to the solo line. In this solo one thirty-second note equals 1/8 of a beat, eight thirty-second notes equal 1 beat.

ILLUSTRATION 7

The ad lib measure then is equal to six quarter notes. When you look at the relationships, you'll see that the thirty-seconds are going to be played faster than the sixteenth notes even when you play the overall rhythm freer. Another benefit of practicing strictly with the metronome is to work out the fingering patterns. In going from the top line "F" to "Bb" to "D", the "Bb" should be fingered with the first finger of the left hand and the first finger of the right hand. This fingering can also be used for the other "Bb" fingerings. Try the following exercise using both "Bb" fingerings. This should help you decide which is easier.

PREPARATION 17

After you get the general feel of the basic rhythm and the correct fingering patterns, play the solo much freer, ad lib.

Measure 50-60   The last phrase of the solo begins in this measure, beginning as it did in the first phrase. When you arrive at measure 53 the tenuto mark and the word "cedez" tell you to give a little extra time to the "F" before going on to the first note of measure 54. In measure 56 there is another ad lib section. As you did before, divide the measure into quarter note beats. Another new rhythm appears in this measure which divides a quarter note into six equal parts. ♩ = ♫♫♫   The complete measure then breaks down into fifteen quarter note beats.

ILLUSTRATION 8

Again work out the rhythms and fingering patterns before playing the solo ad lib. To help your accompanist, give a slight up-down motion with the bell of your instrument to cue the "A" in measure 57. Crescendo on the "A" in measure 57 and begin to slow down in measure 58. Descrecendo on the last note and indicate the cut-off to your accompanist on beat 2 of measure 60.

Andante

Alexandre Beon

Rondo Allegretto

musical terms

sfz   sforzando, forced, giving a strong accent

Johann Baptist Wanhal was one of the earliest composers to write for the clarinet. An original editon of this Sonata, published in 1806 by Simrock in Bonn, can be found in the Library of Congress under the title: <u>Sonata per il clavicembalo o pianoforte con clarinetto o violino obligato.</u> As the original title indicates the solo part could be played on the violin as well as the clarinet. Many publishers would print their music for several different solo instruments.

Wanhal lived most of his life in the eighteenth century — the age of "Classicism"; consequently his music portraits the characteristics of that period: clarity, balance, lyricism, and restraint of emotional expression. The sonata was the most important form of the Classical era. It was usually written for solo instrument and keyboard accompaniment, consisting of four varied movements. This "Rondo Allegretto" is the last movement of Wanhal's <u>Sonata</u>. "Allegretto" means moving, but not too fast and "rondo" refers to a movement consisting of one prominent theme which appears over and over again in alternation with other contrasting themes. It is in cut-time, two beats to a measure, and the suggested tempo is ♩=108. Of course the tempo will depend upon your ability to perform the solo. If you need to slow the tempo somewhat, you should. The following exercises in the key of C will help you prepare for this solo. Practice them using a metronome set at different tempos and using different articulations.

PREPARATION 18

PREPARATION 19

PREPARATION 20

Measure 1-7 The piano begins by stating the "rondo" theme. Study the accompaniment and solo parts carefully to know how the theme begins, the style of the piano part, and what happens when the solo enters.

Measure 8-16 As a contrast to the accompaniment's dynamic level (piano), the solo should begin at forte. Throughout the solo watch the articulations very carefully. For instance, the four eighth notes at the end of measure 8 are slurred, but not the quarter note that follows them in measure 9. The staccato quarter notes should be separated, but not too short.

Measure 20-26 Put your clarinet in your mouth a little early. This will allow you to moisten your reed, draw away excess moisture from your mouthpiece, and take your breath. The first note of measure 21 should be short, as if it were being tossed away.

The second half of beat 1 has a new marking. "Sfz" is the abbreviation for "sforzando" or forced. Therefore, the notes with this marking should be given special emphasis. The force should be created by the air, not by hitting the reed with the tongue. Measure 23 is the beginning of a four measure crescendo. Grow gradually louder making each measure drive towards the next measure and following the articulation exactly as written.

Measure 27-38 Count and think eighth notes during measure 26, then indicate the downbeat of measure 27 to your accompanist with a slight nod of the clarinet. This way, the beat is counted, felt, and seen. Practice the passage from measure 27 to measure 30 slowly with a metronome. As you master the evenness at the slower tempo, the speed should gradually be increased. You should also practice this part with your accompanist so it is unison. Be sure both the solo and accompaniment are balanced, heard equally. The high "D" in measure 30 should be short. In measure 32 the right little finger should not be used on the "C♯" and should be used on the "E" and "D". Practice the following exercise to learn this fingering pattern. These are triplets which divide the quarter note into three equal parts. It may help to think of this rhythm by counting "Trip-le-it." Start with the metronome set at a slow speed and repeat each measure three or four times.

PREPARATION 21

When you play this three-note figure in the solo at measures 31-35, make the quarter notes short as if they were written. The first "F" of measure 35 should be short, but the "F" in the accompaniment has a fermata and should be held a little longer. The accompanist should pause slightly before playing the four eighth note pick-ups which begin your measures of rest.

Measure 39-44 This is the first time the main theme re-appears in the rondo.

Measure 45-67 Decrescendo from measure 45 into measure 47 where the mood and the theme changes to a sustained, lyrical expressivity. Keep counting in these measures even though the note values are longer. Listen to the octaves being played on every beat in the accompaniment. As in Baroque music, the appoggiatura in Classical music would receive one-half or two-thirds the value of the note it precedes. In this solo the appoggiaturas would be played as two eighth notes.

ILLUSTRATION 9

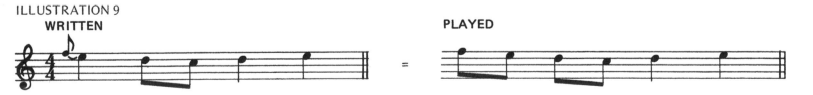

In the section from measures 57-62 be careful to count, even though there are longer note values.

Measure 68-78 In measure 71 keep the right hand down for smoothness. The clarinetist becomes the accompanist starting in measure 73. This figure, outlining the chord, is called an "Alberti bass". Alberti was a harpsichord player and composer of the 18th century who did not invent this figure but often used it. Keep this eighth note figure soft and even.

Measure 78-86   With the pick-ups to measure 79 the clarinetist and pianist have the same rhythm, the two eighth notes and a short quarter note. This time the quarter notes should be tongued. Begin this section with a full rich sound and decrescendo to measure 82. To close out this phrase, pause slightly before the fermata note and before the accompaniment part in measure 86.

Measure 91-96   Match the dynamic level at the end of the accompaniment's decrescendo for your entrance. Use your resonant fingering for the "A" on beat 2 of the measure. Keep the line moving by building the "C" in measure 92. The phrase should move from measure 91 all the way to the last note in measure 96.

Measure 101-106   This is a repetition of the same phrase. Watch the dynamics carefully.

Measure 112-123   Count very carefully through this passage. In measure 116 aim for the high "C" on the second beat by playing a slight crescendo on the eighth notes at the beginning of the measure. The slur from high "D" to "G" in measure 118 will be easier if you'll "pop" the first finger of your left hand down when you play the "G". Even though the last note of this phrase, measure 123, should be played forte, try to decrescendo just slightly so the sound will not be chopped off.

Measure 124-137   Listen for the accompanist's two eighth note pick-ups in preparation for your entrance. Hold the accents on measure 127 and 128 for their full value. A slight separation should be heard in the accompaniment, which has continuous movement in both measures. You should give the cut-off for the fermata note in measure 130. Again your accompanist can put a slight pause before starting with the eighth note pick-ups in this measure.

Measure 138-173   Beginning in this measure the solo part is a repeat of the beginning section. Use the same techniques that were discussed at the beginning.

Measure 174-186   The quarter note — eighth note figure must be played precisely against the accompaniment's moving eighth notes. Emphasize the quarter note with a slight decrescendo on the eighth note - ♩ ♪ ⅞ . Lower the dynamic level in measure 180 so you can crescendo more effectively in measure 181. Make the first note of measure 185 short and the fermata note forceful. Hold a little longer than the actual value, cue the first note of measure 186 which is also short. Play the fermata note forceful but a little longer this time. There should be a definite pause before measure 187. You'll need to cue both the cut-off of measure 186 and the first note of measure 187.

Measure 187-191   Immediately start softly in this phrase. Make this contrast very noticeable and play these five measures softly and expressionless.

Measure 195-205   In measure 201 put a small space before the long note (the syncopated note "C") and a slight accent to emphasize the syncopation. Be sure to use the right little finger on the high "D's".

Measure 207-212   This last section should not slow down at all. Prepare for measure 207 — draw the moisture out of the mouthpiece and take your breath in plenty of time for the entrance. The rhythm in these measures is new. If the beat is subdivided into four eighth notes the sixteenth notes come on the fourth part of the beat. Use the breath to accent the long notes marked with *sfz*. Try the following exercise slowly to get the feel of the division and articulation. Later try it up to the tempo of the solo. In the first two measures, only an **eighth** note is written on the fourth part of the beat. In the other two measures, the eighth is divided into two sixteenths as in the solo.

PREPARATION 22

Keep your embouchure relaxed but firm and the air moving through the instrument.

Listen carefully in measures 209-212. The accompaniment has eighth notes and your quarter notes must be precise. The last two quarter notes should be long, accented and separated with a slight delay before the last note.

Rondo Allegretto

Johann Wanhal
(1739-1813)

Revery and Dance

musical terms

lento   **slow**
con alcuna licenza   **with a little license, freedom**
morendo   **Italian for dying, diminuendo or decrescendo**

new notes

F
(alternate)

"Revery" is a dream-like, fanciful piece. As the tempo direction indicates, it should be slow with a little liberty in the rhythm. This is sometimes called rubato which comes from the Italian "robbed". The tempo is flexible with slight accelerandos (speeding up) and ritards and freedom of expression. As in the ad lib sections of "Andante", work out the basic rhythm first with the metronome. Later work with your accompanist with a more rubato feeling.

This solo is written to display the chalameau register of the instrument. The dynamic level stays quite soft, so the pitch could have a tendency to be sharp. Be sure to play with lots of breath support and a relaxed, but firm embouchure to keep the tone full and rich.

Measure 1-6   Your accompanist must be careful of the clef changes throughout these two selections. For instance, measure 1 begins in the treble clef for both hands. Later the accompaniment moves to both clefs. On your entrance in measure 3 play at a dynamic level of "piano" but keep it balanced with the chord in the accompaniment. Your melodic line should be in tempo and not hurried. It may help to think of these eighth notes as if they had weight or were being stretched. Because an ascending line gives a sensation of a crescendo, don't put any extra crescendo or decrescendo in this first phrase. In measure 4, it is impossible to use the chromatic fingering for "F#". When you move from the "F#" to "F", be very careful that the fingers are exactly coordinated, so no extra notes will be heard. Take a breath after the "F#" only if absolutely necessary. Be sure to use the left little finger for the "C" in measure 5. Listen very carefully to the accompaniment in measures 6 and 7. It will establish the tempo for your entrances in measures 7 and 8.

Measure 7-13   The melody should be played sweetly, softly and delicately. In measure 8 use the left little finger for the "B". It might be best to take the breath in measure 9 even though it is in parentheses. All "Eb's" in this solo should be played with the right index finger on the lowest side key.

Measure 14-18   Breathe! Beginning in measure 14 there is a notated accelerando — each figure is faster than the previous one. There is a new rhythm in this passage — a quintuplet which divides the beat into five equal parts. Practice the following exercises metrically. Be careful that all figures are evenly spaced within the beat.

PREPARATION 23

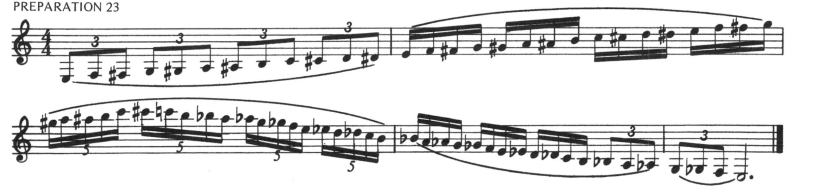

After you've worked out the rhythms and the fingering patterns, free the rhythm so it will not sound too mechanical. Crescendo slightly on the ascending melody as this is the peak of the solo. Stretch the eighth notes for their full value or longer in measure 16 and use the chromatic fingering for the "F♯". Drive the long "B♭" to the "C♯" in measure 17 with more intensity in the tone. If needed, a quick breath can be taken before the "C♯".

Measure 18-24   Use resonant fingerings for the "A" and "B♭" in measure 19 and the chromatic fingering for the "F♯" in measure 20. For the low "F" in measures 22 and 23 use the left little finger. The passage from measure 17 should give the feel of a decrescendo, the effect of winding down after the peak in measure 16. Be sure to hold the low "E" for its full value to the first beat of measure 25.

Measure 24-34   From measure 24 the solo returns to the delicate dream-like quality that was used in the opening. Notice the duet effect between the solo and accompaniment parts. When one part is moving, the other is sustained. The moving part is the more important and should be a little stronger. For the low "F♯" in measure 30 and 33 use the right little finger. Slow down and get softer in the last two measures. The sound should "die away". In playing pianissimo, the "A" may have a tendency to go sharp. Keep the breath support constant and try putting the third finger on the ring only of the "G" hole.

musical terms

sempre	always
adagio	slowly
poco a poco	little by little
accel.	accelerando — becoming faster
maestoso	majestic

The "Dance" was composed to demonstrate another facet of the clarinet by the use of Near Eastern rhythms and modes. This is quite chromatic and should be played lightly and cheerfully, reminiscent of the wind instruments heard in this region.

Measure 1-9   Begin softly with a light bouncy staccato. "Sempre" tells you it should always be soft until the next dynamic marking is shown. Be very careful to play the articulation markings exactly as they are written. In measure 3 play the "B" with the right little finger, "C" with the left and then right little finger for the "E♭". In addition, the "E♭" should be cut off using the tip of the tongue. Think of the syllable "ut" on this eighth note.

PREPARATION 24

The same type of rhythmic figure occurs in measures 5, 6, and 7. In measure 6 it may be easier and more coordinated if you will play the "C" with the left little finger, "C♯" with the right. This keeps the movement from "C♯" to "E" in the right hand. Starting in measure 5 there is a sequence. That is, the same rhythms, articulations and intervals are used but each measure starts a half step higher than the preceding.

Measure 9-10   Be very careful in counting measures 9-10. In measure 10 a change of meter occurs so an extra beat is added. In addition the rhythm is syncopated so the accents fall on the "and" in some cases.

Measure 11-18   Beginning in this phrase accent the notes marked. The syncopation will stand out much more if these are played. Keep the right hand down when moving from the "C-A-C". Whenever notes are followed by an accented note, they should be very short as if plucked away. The eighth notes in the accompaniment should also be very short and dry-sounding. Use the left little finger for "C" in measures 16 and 17. Push plenty of air through the clarinet in this forte passage and keep your throat opened and relaxed.

Measure 19-28 The accompaniment has the melody line for a few measures. Play your part softly enough for the piano to be heard. On each "B" space slightly, reattack firmly, and then let the note decrescendo. In measures 22, 24 and 26 remember to play the grace notes quickly ahead of the beat with the accent on the principle note. Even though this section is slurred, these grace notes will have to be tongued to be heard. Play the "B's" with the right little finger and the "C's" with the left little finger in measures 27 through 30.

PREPARATION 25

Ahead of the beat   On the beat

Measure 29-36 In measure 31 the meter changes from 2/4 to 4/4. The basic quarter note stays the same, just add two beats to each measure. The notes in measures 31 and 32 may sound extremely dissonant, but this is the composer's intent. Play with a full, rich sound to accent this dissonance. The resolution (relief) comes on the "Bb" in measure 33 which is one of the notes in the piano chord. The "Bb" is concert "Ab", the enharmonic tone of "G#" in the piano. From measure 34 the clarinetist must decrescendo and ritard. Be sure to use the chromatic fingering for "Bb" in measure 34. On the fourth beat of measure 34 the "Bb-G" is a tremolo. It is played by alternating two notes as rapidly as possible. Try the following exercise to familiarize yourself with the fingered tremolo.

PREPARATION 26

After the first beat, finger the first note of the tremolo and move only the third finger of your left hand to make the sound change. The tremolo ends on the first beat of measure 36 and the "Bb" is held until the sound dies away.

Measure 37-45 Pause a few seconds before starting with the "a tempo" in measure 37. Remember this means the tempo returns to ♩=128 and the meter returns to 2/4. The melody is the same as it was at the beginning except it is very soft, slurred, and one octave lower. This produces a mysterious, dreamy sound. Because it is so soft a maximum amount of breath support will be needed. If you need to take a breath before the eight measure phrase is finished, take a quick one at the end of measure 40. Play the "F#'s" in measures 38 and 40 with the right little finger.

Measure 45-64 The accompaniment has the same change of meter and syncopation as in measure 9-11. The clarinet also picks up the same rhythm but with different notes, starting a major third higher. This is called modulation, changing keys. The basic techniques will be the same as measures 11-48. The "C#'s" in measure 47 and 49 should be played with the right little finger. The accompaniment chords should be short and accented. Beginning in measure 57 you have exactly the same part as you did in measure 21.

Measure 65-69 The change of tempo starts in measure 65 in the solo part. The quarter note beat starting at measure 65 is equal to two quarter notes in the section immediately before the adagio. When you start, think two beats on each quarter rest or note to get the rhythm set in your mind. The figures in measures 68 and 69 speed up with each succeeding beat, there is also some acceleration within each beat. With the acceleration, there is also a crescendo to the trill in measure 69 which should be a full forte.

Measure 70-77 The soloist must cue the accompanist for the downbeat of measure 70. From that point until the soloist re-enters, the accompanist must set the original tempo of ♩=128. Maestoso indicates the style of the music should be dignified, stately and majestic. The sound is full with slight spacing between notes. When you re-enter in measure 72, imitate the style your accompanist has been playing —long, full-valued notes with accents. In measure 73 play a pronounced ritard ending with a dramatic pause after the fourth beat of the measure. Cue the accompanist with an up-down motion of the bell of your clarinet. The accompanist must play the last three measures very loud, short, accented, and rhythmic. The composer has built a ritard in the rhythms. The quintuplet is slower than the seven notes preceding it and should be played at a steady beat. A slight separation should be put before the last note, which is played long and full without any decrescendo. You will give the cut-off.

Revery

To Ramon Kireilis

Normand Lockwood
(1906-2002)

Dance

fingering chart

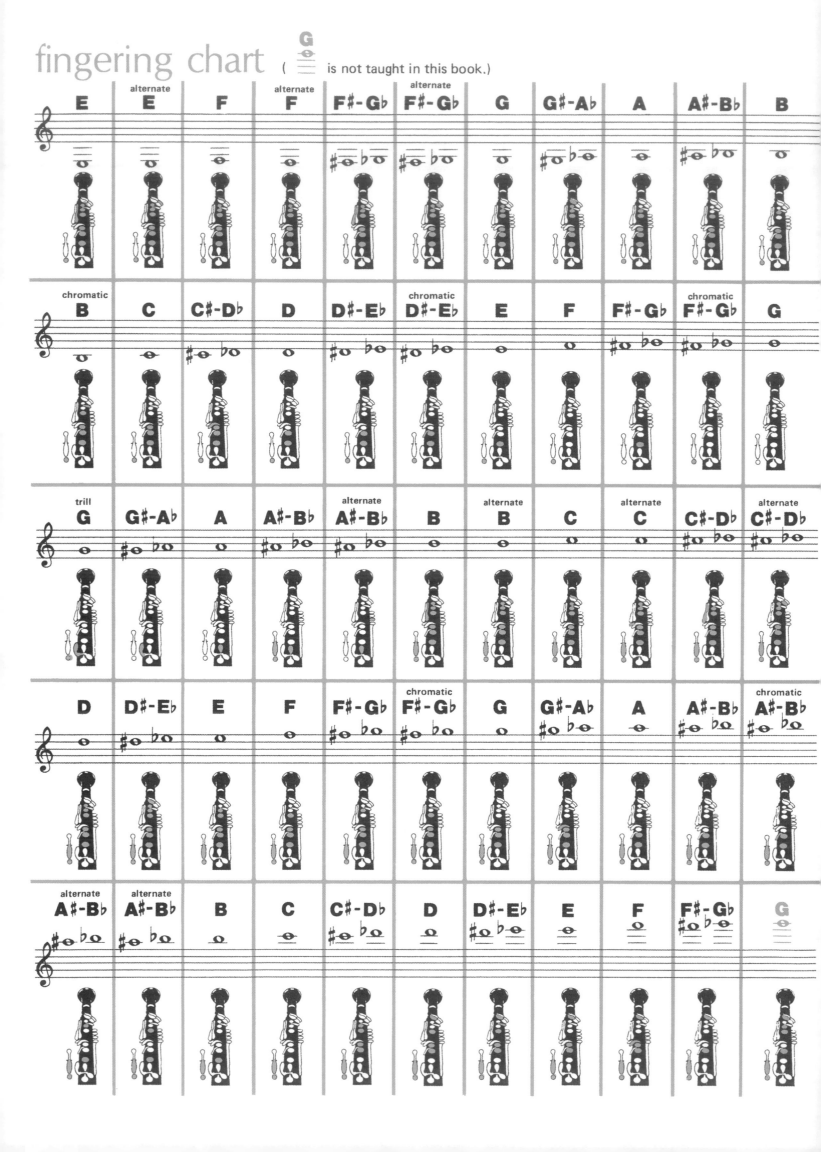